Three Essays on Universal Law

Three Essays on Universal Law

The Laws of Karma, Will and Love

Michael A. Singer

Shanti Publications

Albert Einstein photograph by H. Landshoff.

Albert Einstein quotation: *Ideas and Opinions* by Albert
Einstein, New York: Crown Publications, Inc. 1954,
p. 40.

Paramahansa Yogananda photograph by permission of Self-
Realization Fellowship, Los Angeles, California.

Paramahansa Yogananda quotation: *The Law of Success* by
Paramahansa Yogananda, Los Angeles: Self-Realization
Fellowship, 1970, p. 11.

Meher Baba photograph by permission of the Meher
Spiritual Center, Myrtle Beach, South Carolina.

Meher Baba quotation: Ram Dass quoting Meher Baba from
the record album *Here We All Are*, Vancouver, Canada:
Yogananda Enterprises.

TWELFTH PRINTING

Printed in the United States of America

L. C. No.: 75-7988
ISBN 10: 0-917042-00-X
ISBN 13: 978-0-917042-00-3

To a very special Teacher and Friend,
Reverend Eloise Page

Acknowledgement

I would like to take this opportunity to thank all those who helped this work attain its finished form. In particular, I think of David Rebmann and Donna Wagner for their help polishing the manuscript, and William Huey of Anhinga Press for his professional assistance in the publication process.

Furthermore, anyone who has taught in a college classroom knows the importance of student interest in shaping the nature and quality of a lecture. Since most of these essays were originally given in lecture form, I extend my sincere appreciation and love to all those students at Santa Fe Community College who opened themselves so fully to these new ideas and put them into practice in their daily lives.

Finally, and most importantly, I give heartfelt recognition to Paramahansa Yogananda for his unending flow of inspiration. The wisdom of this great Teacher forms the guidance behind all my constructive thoughts and actions.

Table of Contents

List of Figures and Photographs

Figures

Photographs

frontispiece — Sombrero Galaxy, Virgo constellation

Image Credit: NASA and The Hubble Heritage Team (STScI/AURA)

> This object lies at a distance of about 40 million light years from Earth. The dark rim is caused by a band of light-absorbing dust in the outer arms of the galaxy. The central bulge is caused by the integrated effect of millions of stars concentrated around the nucleus.

verso, The Law of Karma — Albert Einstein, 1946, Princeton, New Jersey

verso, The Law of Will — Paramahansa Yogananda, 1952, Last Birthday at Mt. Washington, California

verso, The Law of Love — Meher Baba, 1938, Alwar India

Introduction

The Westerner who is just beginning to turn his mind inward in search of the deeper Truths finds himself in an interesting situation. He finds that he is so intellectually biased that his intellect itself is responsible for a major portion of his mental unrest. This means that a person who has become stimulated by the depths of the Eastern Teachings has to decide what to do with this overfed intellect.

If we take a look at those around us, it appears that most Western truth seekers have pursued one of two extreme courses of action. The first group are those who tend to intellectually devour all of the spiritual teachings which they come into contact with, but instead of digesting and practicing them, they keep them at an intellectual level. The inevitable result of this course of action is to allow EGO to thrive by taking endless delight in philosophical discussions.

The second group of seekers are those who believe that since the Truth is beyond the mind, the intellect cannot in any way aid us in attaining our Goal. Those who adhere to this belief attempt to abandon the use of their intellect altogether, never allowing the finite mind to expand and perfect itself by reaching out toward the Infinite.

Undoubtedly, the seeker who abandons his intellect has a far better chance of attaining his Goal than the one who attempts a purely intellectual understanding of transcendental teachings. If we look closely, however, we will see that all of the great spiritual teachings have stressed one point in common—*The Path is a Balance:*

> But for earthly needs
> Religion is not his who too much fasts
> Or too much feasts, nor his who sleeps away
> An idle mind; nor his who wears to waste
> His strength in vigils. Nay, Arjuna! call
> That the pure piety which most removes
> Earth-aches and ills, where one is moderate
> In eating and in resting, and in sport;
> Measured in wish and act; sleeping betimes,
> Waking betimes for duty.*

This quotation from the *Bhagavad-Gita* emphasizes the balance which should be reached in dealing with bodily actions such as eating, working, and sleeping. But the same Law of Balance holds for mental and emotional actions as well. Once we direct our lives toward the Inner Path we quickly realize that this achievement of balance is one of the most difficult tasks we can undertake. As such, we must learn to wisely employ *all* of the tools which have been put at our disposal. Since the intellect is recognized to be one of the most developed aspects of the modern Westerner, great efforts should be taken in order to find the balanced use of this mental tool.

*Bhagavad-Gita (The Song Celestial), translated by Sir Edwin Arnold, Wheaton, Ill.: The Theosophical Publishing House, 1970, p. 48-49.

One means of attaining this balance is to study spiritual writings which challenge the intellect as deeply as non-spiritual literature has in the past. In this way the intellect comes to see the spiritual precepts as reasonable alternatives to traditional Western thought. In an attempt to offer a work which employed the intellect to these ends, our first book, *The Search for TRUTH*,* was written. In that work we built an analytical model of man and his relation to the Universe. By properly employing the tool of logic, we step-by-step worked our way deep into the recesses of our innermost being in search of man's true nature. Having explored this inner Universe, we then called upon our storehouse of scientific knowledge in order to explore the true nature of the external Universe. In the end, our intellectually structured analysis clearly pointed to the existence of a Superior Force (called Conscious Energy) which underlies all of Creation. We showed that when viewed from the proper perspective all of the diverse Western sciences, as well as the Eastern and Western religious philosophies, are merely viewing different aspects of this One Underlying Truth.

As discussed above, works such as these help us to see the true spiritual value of our intellects. If we steadfastly study such logical alternatives to our old way of thinking, the mind will become programmed into a frame which is more congenial with spiritual growth. And if we are really sincere in our aspirations,

*Michael A. Singer, *The Search for TRUTH*, Alachua, Fla.: Shanti Publications, 1974.

the resulting quieting of the mind will far outweigh any spiritual pride which might develop. Thus, when properly used, the intellect can be a means to the End. It need not be beaten down, nor need it be so attached to EGO's control that it tricks us into "spiritual pride."

Taking this point a step farther, it should be recognized that this balance for the intellect is really the proper attitude which should be attained for the mind in general. Most aspirants find their mind in such a frenzy that they automatically see it as their worst enemy. They believe that the mind must be beaten before any spiritual progress can come about. But, interestingly enough, those who have really made head-way along the Inner Path have come to see that once the proper mental attitude is reached, the mind can be a dear friend.* *Just because the state of Enlightenment lies beyond the mind does not mean that the mind should be viewed as a hindrance on the Path.* The true aspirant fully uses his body, emotions, and mind in order to help him toward his Goal. The lower aspects of man are only a barrier when they are allowed to work for their own, habit-formed desires. They become the aspirant's dearest friend when they are employed in spiritual pursuits.

It is in this spirit that the current work, *Three Essays on Universal Law*, has been written. In many respects this work builds upon the foundation laid in

*See: Swami Muktananda, *Chitshakti Vilas (The Play of Consciousness)*, Ganeshpuri, India: Shree Gurudev Ashram, 1972, pp. 41-45.

The Search for TRUTH. Nevertheless, great efforts have been made to assure that each essay stands on its own. The reader who studies these Laws with one eye focused on the pages and the other eye focused within himself will gradually notice a framework emerging around which he can structure the seemingly unconnected events of his life. Each reader is invited to study these Higher Laws with the same intellectual skepticism which is characteristic of non-spiritual, academic studies. *Nothing in these pages should be blindly accepted.* Since the three Laws presented in this work play a major role in governing our everyday lives, if they are Truth, they should be able to stand the test of daily observation in the Laboratory of Life. The greatest end which this work can serve is to stimulate us to turn our intellects, now overburdened with solving life's problems, toward solving the mysteries of life itself.

THE
LAW
OF
KARMA

The Law of Karma

The scientist's religious feeling takes the form of a rapturous amazement at the harmony of natural law, which reveals an intelligence of such superiority that, compared with it, all the systematic thinking and acting of human beings is an utterly insignificant reflection....

—Albert Einstein

Karma and Modern Science

The entire Universe is aptly described as one, tremendously complex system in a state of dynamic equilibrium. The order and intricate balance of the Cosmic Structure are literally beyond the scope of man's limited intellect. In every direction which scientific minds probe, they unfailingly discover laws governing the operations of the Universal System. For example, if we delve into the macrocosmic area we are confronted with the overwhelming balance which structures the relative positions, shapes of orbits, and rates of velocity of all the celestial bodies in the millions of galaxies.

To begin to get an idea of how exact the order of the macrocosmic structure is, we can take a look at the fascinating manner in which the planet Neptune was discovered. Two physicists, Le Verrier in France and John Couch Adams in England, had independently come to the conclusion that in accordance with the calculated forces in action, there was an unexplained influence on the orbits of the planets in our solar system. In order to explain the behavior of the system as a whole, they mathematically calculated this unexplained variable and hypothesized the location of another, yet to be discovered planet. On the same night as receiving Le Verrier's calculations at the observatory in France, astronomers located Neptune, the eighth planet of the system. It was almost exactly where mathematical calculations had positioned it. And the entire Cosmic Structure is ordered to this same degree, though many of the influencing forces are yet to be discovered because of their distance from us in space.

However, it is not just the macrocosmic structure which displays this phenomenal balance and order. The physicist probing the secrets of the atomic and sub-atomic worlds finds the same adherence to basic laws. For example, a major part of the science of chemistry is based upon atoms behaving in a given, consistent manner according to the laws governing their electron rings. Even when studying energy itself, physicists note an adherence to the "Law of Least Expenditure of Energy." Thus, there is a given order governing the behavior of the energy, the atoms, the molecules, and the complex molecular chains such that laws can be framed to explain all observed activity.

Furthermore, viewing these molecular structures as they combine to compose the world of our everyday sense-life, we again see no end to the prevalence of balance and order. On this planet Earth there is a very complex "balance of Nature" (i.e., ecological balance). It includes not only the individual ecological system of any pond or forest, but also the complex structure which ties together all features of the mineral, plant, and animal kingdoms. As if this were not mind shaking enough, it is also true that this entire ecological balance is affected by weather conditions and lunar positions, which are, in turn, intricately tied in to the entire macrocosmic balance discussed earlier. What is more, since all component parts of the ecological system are composed of atoms, we can see that this "balance of Nature" is totally dependent upon the order of the microcosmic system as well as the macrocosmic. So we must conclude that the entire Universe, from the infinite stretches of the macrocosmic down to the infinitesimal units of the microcosmic, is *one inter-related system*. This system displays a degree of order and balance which is far beyond our intellectual comprehension. Each time the order has appeared to breakdown under the increasing sophistication of scientific research, we have always found subtler laws in operation. The closer we get to the underlying forces at work, the more consistent and reliable are the laws revealed.

Perhaps most of us feel that we are already quite familiar with the degree of order which characterizes the Universe around us. In fact, it may be that the above discussion appears a bit overdrawn. But a very interesting facet of man's intellectual perception of life is that he easily notes the perfection of balance above and below him, but he rarely takes time to have a close look at his own relation to this balance. It is to this task that we devote the present essay: To analyze man's position in the Universal Order.

We can begin to explore this complex relation between man and Nature by noting that the perfect systems which comprise our bodies are but one input into the ecological balance. As such, these internal physiological systems are governed by the universal macrocosmic-microcosmic equilibrium system. Our respiratory system is tied in intricately to the atmospheric balance, our digestive system is affected by (and affects) vegetation conditions, and, thus, our physiological being is totally dependent upon an infinite number of external variables. Furthermore, it is not solely our physiological aspect which is affected by the world around us. The specific patterns of our emotions and thoughts also are dependent upon the events facing us in the outside world.

But what about these external events themselves? After all that has been said concerning the perfect balance and order of the entire Universal Structure, can we now argue that the events which take place in our everyday lives are "random" in nature? In fact, in the scope of formal equilibrium analysis, can there be such a thing as a "random event" in an equilibrium system? By definition, a dependent event cannot be random, and all events within a system are, to a greater or lesser extent, dependent upon all other events. Thus, to argue that "luck" or "chance" has had any effect on one's life is totally unscientific. It denies the balance and order which science has found permeating the Universal Structure, from macrocosm right down to microcosm.

What, then, is the order which underlies the pattern of our lives and directs us from one dependent event to another? We find that in Eastern philosophy it is called the Law of Karma, or the Law of Cause and Effect. As we delve into the workings of this law we will find its universality almost renders the analysis simplistic. Nevertheless, it must be remembered that it is the Law of Karma which forms the missing link between the scientifically discovered order of the Universe external to man, and the events which comprise man's varied experiences in life.

The first important point in our analysis is to note that Cause and Effect is the most basic of all of the universal laws. A moment of individual reflection will show us that this law forms the foundation for the law of gravity, Darwin's law of natural selection, the law of diminishing returns, and all other relationships which have been discovered by all scientists of all times. In fact, the Law of Karma is so basic and so universal that it is generally overlooked as the fundamental law of Creation. Perhaps the best way to see how basic and universally prevalent this law is, is to stop and realize that it does not *have* to be in operation. That is, the Cosmos could be filled with atoms which behaved in a completely random manner, unstructured by any order of any kind. In this fictitious world (if one can even imagine it) we could carry out an experiment, scientifically observe the results, and yet the same experiment might never yield identical results twice. It is most difficult for our intellects even to conceive of this, for we are so fixed in thinking in terms of Cause and Effect. But this process of Cause and Effect is merely a law, a particular order which structures Creation. It is *not* an intrinsic quality of the underlying energy field. *Cause and Effect is just a particular system of order which governs the behavior of the energy field.* Once we recognize Cause and Effect as the most basic universal law, as opposed to a "truism" to be overlooked, we have made a major advance toward understanding the structure and meaning of life.

Undoubtedly we need not belabor the point that all of science is based upon this fundamental law. Let it suffice to say the very fact a scientist sets out to explain an observed event means he believes there is a sequential chain of causes behind that event. Our main interest here, however, is to show that this same Law of Karma which governs all scientifically observed events also governs the events of our everyday lives.

Let us begin with a rather simple example: that of an accident at a crossroads where the stop light was out of order. In such cases we immediately think, "What bad luck I have, I never get the breaks." The idea that it was not an "accident" at all, for there can be no such thing as an "accident" in a system governed by an unfailing law, appears almost ludicrous. Yet the event

in question was obviously not a "random" event.
Think of all of the causes behind your being at the
street corner the exact moment as the other car. And
the causes behind the broken light, and those which
determined the behavior of the other driver, and so on.
We cannot just take a moment in time, pretending it
exists independent of the rest of the system. All events
are merely links in an infinite, universal chain of Cause
and Effect. *Every single occurrence is the essential out-
come of all of the causative factors operating within the
system.* And these causative factors stretch as far back
into time and space as we care to trace them.

It is important to note that this also holds true for
all of life's "special events," such as first meeting loved
ones, having children, inheriting large sums of money,
or getting fired from a job only to fall upon an unbe-
lievable career opportunity. It is all part of an inter-
related system of Cause and Effect—not a single facet
can be attributed to luck or chance. However, at this
point some may feel that if the causes are so far
removed from a man's control, they might as well be
random. But this line of thinking exists because we
have only begun to scratch the surface of the Universal
Law of Karma.

This purely physical operation of karma explains
only a small part of our lives. In order to expand our
understanding of the events which face us each day, we
must realize that Cause and Effect is not arbitrary in its
operation. There is actually a phenomenal "equity" in
the application of this universal law. By the very

nature of the law's mode of operation, the effect always exerts its influence back onto the cause in an exact proportion to the original strength of the cause. *That is, in the Newtonian sense, for every action there is an equal and opposite reaction.*

For example, if we roll one marble into a stationary one, we can say that the behavior of the first was the "cause," and the resultant behavior of the second the "effect." But we also know that the first marble did not continue on its way unaffected by the results of its own action. The course of the first marble was altered decisively in both direction and velocity in proportion to the effect it had on the second marble's course. This, indeed, is seen to be perfect equity. And this equitable quality of the Law of Cause and Effect is operative throughout the Universe. It is "how" the law implements itself, and, as such, holds true wherever the law is in operation.

In this respect the relationship is analogous to the law of gravity which implements itself based upon the relative mass of the objects in question. The difference being that the Law of Cause and Effect (Karma) implements itself such that the cause of an event reaps the effects of that event in exactly the proportion that it originally contributed to the occurrence of the event. Such is the Law of Karma. Thus, a man exerting enough force in his arms to lift a 100 pound weight, simultaneously has an exactly opposite vector force of 100 pounds tending to push his arms down. Even from the perspective of physics we see that the "cause" which sows the seeds of an action will always receive the compensating fruits of that action. This equitable aspect of the Law of Karma is often referred to as the Law of Compensation.

Another important feature of the Law of Karma is that it is in operation at all levels of Creation, not just in the world of matter. The science of psychology teaches that emotions and thoughts also are governed by Cause and Effect. Here we say that our long run emotional patterns are governed by childhood experiences, and that our volatile short run feelings are caused by both outside events and inner thought patterns. So the intricate relation of Cause and Effect which ties external events to our thought and emotional patterns means that these non-physical aspects of our being are tied to the universal chain of Cause and Effect analyzed earlier. *It is all one system.* The entire Universe at the physical, emotional, and mental planes is an interrelated structure governed by the Law of Cause and Effect.

However, as obvious as the application of the Law of Karma is to these higher aspects of our being, the question remains regarding the equity aspect of the law. At first glance it is hard to see an unfailing operation of a Law of Compensation concerning our thoughts and emotions. In order to reveal the operation of this law, let us work with a few examples. First, we have all had situations where we were hateful toward a person and our behavior caused the feeling to be reciprocated. Furthermore, at times we have become angry and lost our tempers, only to generate a similar reaction from other individuals. There are obviously numerous examples of such immediate operations of the compensation aspect of karma. But, again, it must be emphasized that it does not *have* to work this way. We are so used to thinking in terms of such "logical" reactions to specific events, that we find it difficult to abstract sufficiently to realize that what we mean by "logical" is merely the operation of the Law of Cause and Effect along with its compensation principle.

But karma does not always operate as immediately as in the above examples. When there is a time lag involved, the operation of the law becomes so obscured that we ignore its presence altogether. An example of a short time lag is seen when we gossip negatively about a person, and the immediate effect is a positive superiority feeling within us. Once the gossip wends its way back to the individual involved, however, we find ourselves receiving the negative fruits of our initial action. Often the lag is so great that we are completely ignorant that we were the ones who initially set the law into operation. Thus, we are always complaining about people's actions toward us, when, in reality, we ourselves lay the pattern for our interpersonal relations.

Evidence of a much longer lag in the operation of the Cause and Effect Principle is seen in the case where we befriend a stranger, and then years later we apply for a job in which he turns out to be the interviewer. It all comes back, without fail. But the fact that the lags can be of any length, and that there are so many sequences of Cause and Effect in operation at any given moment, make the application of this unalterable law so obscured that "randomness" appears to be the case.

What we shall see is that this is just the beginning. In every example given above we at least are able to trace a physical transmission mechanism by which the law was carried out. Actions taking place on the physical plane worked their way through Cause and Effect by means of particular interpersonal relations. But the law is much broader than this. As pointed out earlier, Cause and Effect governs the operation of the emotional and mental planes as well as the physical. Thus, we can set karmic patterns into operation with both cause and effect being worked out at the higher levels.

Perhaps the simplest example of this process is the person who goes through life emitting very high vibrations at the emotional level. Since mere contact with these vibrations causes others to feel "high," this person finds that wherever he is, happiness dominates his external environment. In contrast, if we go around harboring negative thoughts and emotions, we invariably find ourselves surrounded by friends who vibrate at approximately the same rate. So, again, we see the Law of Cause and Effect in operation—we are reaping the fruits of our own negative thoughts and emotions. Yet in these cases the transmission mechanism for the law is directly via the interchange of emotional vibrations, and, thus, no physical mode of transmission is necessary. Furthermore, as with the examples given earlier, there are time lags prevalent in the operation of

Cause and Effect carried out at the higher levels.

So now, taking into consideration all of the "causes" which we generate on the mental, emotional, and physical planes, we begin to get an idea of how many "effects" are being worked out simultaneously. This is the reason we can commit a negative act and appear to receive positive results. The strongest karmic patterns always will take preeminence, and the currently sown seeds will have to wait their round to be worked out.

Looking again to Eastern philosophy, we find that these yet to be worked out seeds of past actions (i.e., the "causes" which have not yet fully satisfied the law by generating the necessary compensating effects) are called *sanskaras*. Each man can be envisioned as guided through life according to the nature of his *sanskaras*, because an uncompleted link in the chain of Cause and Effect is as unnatural to the order of Creation as a ball thrown into the air which is yet to come back down. A tremendous force is created in order that the action be completed, and the law satisfied. One might easily think of this in terms of the force acting upon all aspects of a system being drawn toward a stable equilibrium point. Just as it is true that the equilibrium force which guides an economic system has the power to direct the particular distribution of pennies, so do these *sanskaras* have the strength to direct the behavior of every atom in Creation, since they are all part of the same Universal System.

It should be emphasized that since these *sanskaras* are merely forces set into action according to the Law of Cause and Effect, there is no single, unique manner in which they must be worked off.* That is, if we hurt someone in a love relationship, we must receive our "equal and opposite reaction." But this does not mean that the same individual must hurt us in the same manner. The *sanskara* can be "burned off" by another individual causing us similar feelings of hurt and grief as we caused our original lover. This is the reason that some people, having a strong *sanskara* to work off, marry partners with specific traits which end up getting them down. However, if they terminate the relationship prior to working out the karmic pattern for which they were drawn together, they continue to project these strong *sanskaras* and will again attract to themselves a spouse with similar underlying traits. This pattern will continue to dominate their marital relations until they fully satisfy their "karmic debt" by learning to get along with people having these traits.

Karma and Predestination

It cannot be stressed enough that these karmic patterns govern every event of our lives. There is no such thing

---

*The intricate workings of karmic law are far beyond the scope of the current analysis. There are many diverse outlets by which any given *sanskara* can be removed. For example, aside from working off karma in the "natural" manners referred to in our analysis, techniques such as repentance and meditation can actually burn off *sanskaras* on the higher levels. For a fairly thorough coverage of karmic law by an Eastern Master, see: Meher Baba, *Discourses*, San Francisco: Sufism Reoriented, Inc., 1967, vol. I, pp. 54-91.

as "chance" in a world governed by Cause and Effect. However, the Law of Karma is something quite different from the doctrine of predestination. In predestination we think in terms of some power, divorced from ourselves, having "written the book" in advance of our own birth. In contrast to this, karma states that we ourselves write our own book, but do so in accordance with the operating principle of the law itself. Karma is not any particular event or set of circumstances, it is merely the iron clad Law of Cause and Effect with its operating principle of equitable compensation. Our actions form the variable input, then the law determines the output. This is obviously far from the already set patterns of predestination.

Turning to Figure 1 (next page) we have a comparative analysis to aid us in understanding this important distinction between karma and predestination. In Figure 1-A (predestination) the solid arrows represent the future directions our lives will take. These directions are all predetermined—fixed by some superior decree. In Figure 1-B (karma) the vertical double line represents an "ordering system" (i.e., the Law of Karma), the dotted lines signify our past and current actions, and the solid arrows again depict the future patterns of our lives. We see from this that karma only "orders" our inputs such that they yield specific outputs. Further, Figure 1-B shows us that in this system of karma not only does each action generate an effect, but the relation between input and output is so ordered and consistent that predictability becomes possible.

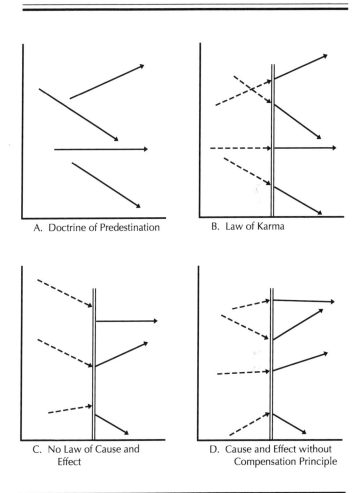

A. Doctrine of Predestination

B. Law of Karma

C. No Law of Cause and Effect

D. Cause and Effect without Compensation Principle

Figure 1—Alternative Universal Ordering Systems

Perhaps the use of this diagram can aid us in driving home the point made earlier that Cause and Effect is only a law, and not a "truism" to be totally ignored. In Figure 1-C we have a hypothetical alternative ordering system in which initiated actions *only sometimes* yield effects, as well as there existing effects which had no causes from within the system itself. Another perfectly plausible alternative universal order is shown in Figure 1-D. This figure depicts a world in which each cause does generate an effect, but "randomness" governs the direction of the effect (i.e., the aspect of equitable compensation is missing). Despite the intellectual recognition of these alternative ordering systems, the fact remains that both scientific research and our own life patterns show beyond any doubt that Figure 1-B best explains the world in which we live. Thus, karma is, at all times, in all circumstances, the law governing the entire pattern of Creation.

Karma and Reincarnation

The analysis thus far has shown beyond any reasonable doubt that Cause and Effect dictates all events within the Universal System. What is more, the analysis has also shown that perfect equity prevails at all times due to the compensation aspect of this universal law. There are still many circumstances in our lives, however, which appear to contradict the operation of karma. For example, where is the cause which determined who our parents would be? Or the cause behind what

positive or negative attributes our bodies and minds
would display? Surely a person born into a wealthy
home with happily married parents is starting off his
life with a series of inputs which place him way ahead
in the Cause and Effect game. If he learns love at
home and is given a good moral and intellectual
education, he begins accumulating "good *sanskaras*"
right from the beginning. These *sanskaras*, in turn, help
to attract good circumstances which tend to perpetuate
positive growth.

Now, it is true that by his daily actions this person
could easily alter this pattern into a negative one. But
beyond any question he certainly was given a head start
over a child born into a poor, militant family. Where,
then, is the equity? And when a child is born blind, or
handicapped in other ways, while another child is given
a shapely body and a beautiful voice—where is the
aspect of compensation? It is incongruous with the
operation of the law to argue that the karma of the
parents *alone* was responsible for these aspects of the
child's physical, emotional, and mental patterns. The
child is an individual entity, and in later life he will be
held responsible for all actions which he initiates.
Thus, unless there is a tremendous flaw in the Law of
Karma there must be some manner in which these very
important, seemingly random childhood conditions are
explained. The Law of Reincarnation is exactly what is
needed to restore the balance of the Universal System.

In order to understand the Law of Reincarnation we
must recognize the individual soul as that aspect of our

being which is "conscious receiver" of all sensory messages sent from the physical, the emotional, and the mental planes.* The soul is the Witness—aware of all activity on each plane, but totally transcending body, emotions, and mind. While the soul is constantly receiving messages from the lower aspects of our being, it becomes identified with these aspects. We then think: "I *am* my body. I *am* my emotions, I *am* my thoughts." It is this "soul," the Pure Consciousness aspect of our being, which is being bound by the process of accumulating and wearing off *sanskaras*. Thus, despite the fact that "You" live in the delusion of ego-consciousness and allow habit-formed patterns of body, emotions, and thoughts to govern your behavior, it is still "You," the individual soul, who are responsible for all of your actions.

With this understanding of the true nature of the soul we are prepared to resume our examination of reincarnation. The first relevant question is: "What happens to all the *sanskaras* of a man lying on his deathbed?" Does the entire Universal Structure cease to operate because the group of atoms comprising the physical body goes through the change called death? The law must be satisfied. After all, karma is the underlying force behind all of Creation. What actually happens is that the soul, "imprinted" with the specific karmic patterns which it accumulated over that lifetime,

*For a thorough analysis of the soul as the "conscious receiver," see: Michael A. Singer, *The Search for TRUTH*, Alachua, Fla.: Shanti Publications, 1974, pp. 9-41.

spends some time in the higher realms, and, then, is reincarnated back into human form. All of the conditions surrounding this birth (such as who the parents are, and what the specific physical and intellectual aspects will be) are determined by the karma of the reincarnating soul. The equilibrium force in operation will attract together individuals and specific worldly conditions such that *sanskaras* can most readily be worked off.

Thus, the doctrine of reincarnation is absolutely necessary in order that the Law of Cause and Effect (with its equitable compensation aspect) be able to operate uninterruptedly. Otherwise, we would have karmic seeds which, due to physical death, would never generate the corresponding fruits. Also, we would have "effects" surrounding the various conditions of birth which would apparently have no equitable "causes." Note that the recognition of life after death, alone, cannot satisfy this break in the law. It does not explain why different souls begin life in such uneven conditions, only to be judged equally by the Law of Cause and Effect throughout life and after death. Where is the equity of two "new souls," one who starts life in a pious family and the other in a poor, angry, uneducated family? Undoubtedly, the strength of the soul can overcome these latter conditions, but it is surely easier to "live right" when born into the pious family.

Furthermore, the Law of Reincarnation not only restores the equity of the system, it also gives us an explanation for "child prodigies." We all recognize that upon death the soul loses its physical body. But it is also true that the emotional and mental aspects, which exist on planes higher than the physical, remain intact. When karmic conditions become right for the next reincarnation, these emotional and mental traits reincarnate along with the soul. Throughout this new incarnation these prenatal qualities will manifest as "aptitudes" for certain activities, as well as intense interest in certain subjects. Advanced souls can even display use of these aspects from previous births at quite an early age, as in the case of Mozart, who composed symphonies at the age of five. So when scientists see a very high correlation between intellectual parents and intellectual children, and then draw the "definite" conclusion that these features are carried genetically, they are being shortsighted. In truth, the cause of this correlation is that intelligent parents tend to "attract" an intelligent soul into the body which their genes have created. This is because they will be able to provide a suitable environment for him to work out his *sanskaras*.

Now we are finally able to see in totality just how complex the structure is which governs our lives. Not only do we have all the *sanskaras* being created at the physical, emotional, and mental levels during each activity of this lifetime (postnatal *sanskaras*), but also the enormous number of variables added due to karmic seeds sown in past lives (prenatal *sanskaras*). Thus, this supremely perfect order of the Universe goes on all

around us. But the Structure is so vast, and our
thinking so ego-centered, that we mistake perfect order
for randomness.

The Law of Karma and the Meaning of Life

The forces in action now have been uncovered sufficiently that we begin to catch a glimpse of the magnif-
icent system which is Creation. But what is the goal
of this system? In what direction are these laws
guiding the structure as a whole? Interestingly enough,
this seemingly abstract philosophical inquiry can be
answered now that we have an understanding of the
Law of Karma. We need merely "step back" and view
our everyday experiences from the soul's point of view,
that of the "Objective Observer."

Once attaining this "Witness" perspective of life, a
definite meaning comes into focus. For example, when
we walk up and touch a hot stove the body gets
burned, and, thus, we learn "a lesson." Or if we stay
up too long without sleep the body gets sick, and,
again, we have been taught "a lesson." This holds true
for staying out in the rain, eating the wrong kinds of
food, staying too long underwater, and so on. By
means of the Law of Cause and Effect, which will
invariably repeat itself given the same conditions, we
learn many "lessons" concerning the care of the body.
For there are certain activities which are in balance
with the use of our bodily tool, while others are not.
Imagine for a moment that there was no one to tell us

about proper care of the body. Still, we would, by
way of experience (i.e., Cause and Effect), soon learn
the do's and don'ts involved. The Law of Cause and
Effect is actually teaching us something—how to come
into balance with the physical plane. If we are slow to
learn, no matter, for the law operates every time we
transgress it. Sooner or later we will learn how to
escape the negative effects and pursue the positive ones.

So a Path is being laid before us which yields the
maximum positive results concerning our relation to the
world of atoms. *In essence, the Law of Cause and
Effect is training the soul, which does not exist on the
physical plane, how to properly operate on the lower
levels of Creation.*

The physical body, however, is only one aspect of
our being. The "Cosmic Schoolteacher," Cause and
Effect, holds classes on the proper care of our emotional and mental aspects as well. When we walk
around hating everyone, we bear the fruits of our
action by living in a cold world full of hate. If we
allow our emotions to go out of control in anger or
lust, we eventually pay the price in accordance to the
karmic law. In contrast, if we remain peaceful and
loving, we walk through life surrounded by these
beautiful vibrations and stay "high" all the time. In
this way we are gradually being taught to come into
balance with our emotional aspect. *There is a Path on
which the soul can walk which is totally frictionless—
filled with Bliss, Love, Peace, and Contentment at all
times.* The Law of Cause and Effect is doing everything
in its power to help us tread this Path.

Furthermore, the same holds true for our mental aspect. If we harbor negative thoughts, they always lead to negativity. Whereas positive thinking is a power which can create a Heaven on Earth. We all know this, for every time we have made the slightest move in the right direction we have been given "a carrot;" while moves in the wrong direction have yielded "the stick." The problem is that due to the time lags involved we often miss the message. We sneak out and cheat on our wives, immediately receiving all of the positive sense gratification. Then, over time, our marital relationship suffers, the wife suffers, and we have created a very negative situation. But the temptation for the short run gain causes us to be blind to the full operation of the universal law in action.

However, karma is the perfect teacher. Patience is one of her greatest virtues. She will give us the same lessons again and again, until we finally learn them. The specific *sanskaras* involved will continue to attract similar circumstances to us, regardless of where we go or what we do. It is for this reason it appears that we constantly are being tempted on our weakest front. These are the lessons we need to learn the most.

What is more, it is clearly evident that despite the fact our specific karmic patterns present each of us with a perfectly tailored classroom, we are all being taught the same Truth. In the end, we are all learning to control body, emotions, and mind so we can realize ourselves as "soul." How long it takes to learn these lessons is really dependent upon the individual's will power—for dynamic will is a present, deliberate action taken by the soul, while daily habits are merely the manifestation of our past karmic patterns. If reason does not guide our will, however, we end up creating more and more negative *sanskaras* to be worked off. But if we consciously and steadfastly exercise our will, attempting to learn the "lessons of Life" more quickly, we will grow much faster than waiting for *sanskaras* to be naturally removed.

Interestingly enough, as we take such positive actions to aid our development, we notice that karma becomes more immediate. That is, all of the lags discussed earlier become shorter, which makes it easier to see the fruits of our present actions. The reason for this increased rapidity of burning off newly created *sanskaras* is as we move along the Path, our collection of *sanskaras* begins to diminish. As we come into tune with universal law, our past debts can be worked off while newly created karma tends to move us in the right direction. As this store of *sanskaras* dwindles, new "causes" of current actions are free to generate their compensating effects. Thus, each step of the Path becomes somewhat easier to take. Since we can see the results of our actions more directly, we are able to adjust our behavior accordingly.

So via the Law of Cause and Effect, *Life is telling us something.* The more prepared we are to exert positive, reason-guided will to receive and comprehend her message, the more quickly we will evolve toward the Ultimate Goal of Life—Self-Realization.

Enlightenment—Beyond the Law of Cause and Effect

When a soul moves far enough along the Path, he comes to realize intuitively that he is totally distinct from body, emotions, and mind. Once he fully identifies himself as Pure Conscious Energy, he transcends all karma. *In the purifying fires of Enlightenment all pre- and postnatal* sanskaras *are burned away.* In order to understand this, we must recognize that karma is essentially an attribute of lower self. Higher Self (soul) is merely the Eternal Witness of the entire process of man's evolution. But when the "soul" falsely identifies with the physical body, it renders itself subject to the Law of Karma operating at this level. The soul then goes through lifetime after lifetime led around by the specific *sanskaras* involved. However, the moment the soul realizes it is not the physical body nor the psychical personality—but that it is Pure Consciousness— it is freed from having to live off the karmic debts.

It should be understood that this instantaneous freedom from all *sanskaras* in no way contradicts the operation of the Law of Karma *in* Creation—for an Enlightened Being has risen *above* Creation. He has merged with the Intelligent Force (Conscious Energy) in Its pure state—prior to Its manifestation as the various planes of Creation. In essence, since all observed "causes" and "effects" are only manifestations of the same underlying Energy Field, *at the Energy level Cause and Effect are One.* Only in the world of Creation does this homogeneous Energy Field take on the characteristics of a diversified Universe whose aspects are ordered by the Law of Cause and Effect. Thus, Enlightenment represents the Ultimate Balance of the system as a whole. The forces of Cause and Effect can reach a no more perfect, permanent equilibrium than when they become One.

It must be remembered that only man, as the highest creature on the evolutionary ladder, has the ability to come directly into Union with the Infinite Source. As he strives toward this end, however, he is aiding the balance of the system as a whole. Each man who consciously puts forth the necessary will power to speed up the process of his evolution is at the same time causing the entire system to evolve more rapidly. To those who see this Truth, and realize the task which lies before them, there is no end to the assistance provided on every step of the Journey. This is the direction all aspects of Creation are leading us, and the entire Universal Balance will aid us in progressing along this Path. In the meantime, knowledge of the universal laws will help us better understand our lives and accept that *It All Happens For The Highest Good. Every event contributes to the balance of the system as a whole.*

So remember the Law of Karma, for it has been written: "As you sow, so then shall you reap."

THE
LAW
OF
WILL

The Law of Will

Every outward manifestation is the result of will, ... The dynamo of all your powers is volition, or will power. Without volition you cannot walk, talk, work, think, or feel. Therefore will power is the spring of all your actions.

— Paramahansa Yogananda

A Model of the Will Force

I felt the urge to hit him right then and there. But, thinking ahead to the consequences, I held myself back.

I don't know why I did it. I had definitely decided not to say anything to her about it. But the moment we were together, the whole story came out. It was practically out of my control.

Explaining the interplay of forces at work behind human behavior is a noble task, indeed. Each of the great scholars in this area has postulated a variety of underlying motives in an attempt to analyze scientifically the actions of men. We have sex theories, fear of death theories, superman theories, and so on. Regardless of which of these modern views on the *impulse behind human behavior* is endorsed, however, there is one thing of which we can all be certain—each man is endowed with a special inner force which potentially allows him total control over his speech, actions, emotions, and thoughts.

We all know that just prior to opening our mouths to speak or moving our bodies to act, there is a brief moment during which we could decide whether or not to allow the action to take place. Most of the time, however, we let this very important moment pass and allow speech and actions to flow automatically. In essence, we allow ourselves to react instinctively to the various stimuli of our outer and inner environments. Nevertheless, at least some of the time we do take advantage of that split second available for rational, reason-guided decision making. When we do this, and then consciously follow the results of this inner decision process, we say we are exercising our own "will." This act of will is obviously in drastic contrast to the stimulus-response mechanism allowed to operate whenever permitting that moment available for inner reflection to pass by.

So we see that will power is an inner force which allows us consciously to take the reins during any given situation, rather than permitting the situation to lead us. It is will power which separates man from all of the merely mechanical conditioned response mechanisms. *Will is the force which can intercede during the lag between stimulus and response, and make it so that any response can manifest, depending upon the desires of the conscious entity exercising the will*. So will is seen to be a very important concept. It is a force which stands in direct opposition to any of the modern theories which attempt to explain human behavior solely on the basis of causative stimuli.

But what exactly is "will?" Where does it come from? How do we manage to have control of this force? What does it mean to "develop" will? The intent of the current essay is to present a Law of Will which should shed light on these generally ignored questions, as well as give us a deeper insight into the power of this force within us.

The first step in developing this analysis is to formulate a model of man to use as a foundation. Such a model has been rigorously developed in a previous work,* and need not be formally supported here. The model is quite straightforward and should pose no difficulty to the unfamiliar reader. Referring to Figure 2 (next page) we see that the most basic aspect of man is his body—the animal self. This is the aspect of our being which exists on, and allows us to become aware of, the physical plane. Above this we have the psychical self. That is, the combination of the emotional and mental aspects of our being. These aspects, being more subtle than the world of atoms, are generally traced back to the astral and mental planes, respectively. In order to simplify the present analysis we shall combine this entire system of man's physical, emotional, and mental aspects, and refer to it as the "lower self." We use the term "lower" not necessarily in a derogatory sense, but merely to denote that these

*Michael A. Singer, *The Search for TRUTH*, Alachua, Fla.: Shanti Publications, 1974, pp. 9-41.

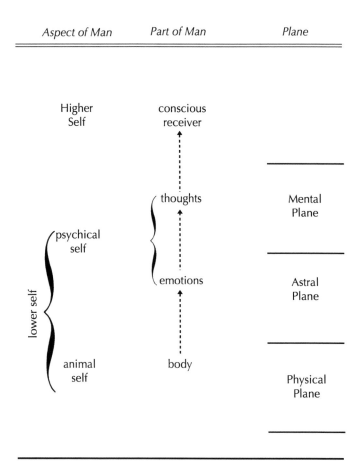

Figure 2—Model of Man

animal and psychical aspects are totally subservient to the aspect analyzed below.

We all know that each day "we" receive messages sent from the physical plane, via the five senses. "We" also receive (i.e., feel) various emotions, as well as become aware of the constant influx of thoughts. But who exactly is this "we," the conscious receiver of all messages sent from the physical, emotional, and mental aspects of our being? Ponder over the questions: "Am I my senses, or am I the receiver of my senses? Am I my emotions, or am I the feeler of my emotions? Am I my thoughts, or am I conscious of my thoughts?" The intuitive affirmation of the second half of each of these questions clearly indicates that there is a "You" in there who is quite distinct from body, emotions, and thoughts. This "You" plays the essential role of conscious receiver of all messages sent from the lower aspects of our being. (See dotted lines in Figure 2.) It is this Pure Consciousness aspect of the system, an aspect totally transcendent of body, emotions, and mind, that we shall refer to as "Higher Self" or "soul."

So the starting point for our analysis of man's will power is with this view of man: A Higher Self of Pure Conscious Energy who is receiver of all stimuli sent from the physical, emotional, and mental aspects of our being; and a lower self with whom we are so identified that we live under the delusion of, "I *am* my body, I *am* my emotions, I *am* my thoughts." When in reality, "You," the consciousness which is right now becoming aware of this sentence as it is read to you by the

"voice" inside your head, *are Pure Consciousness*—
totally transcendent to body, emotions, and mind.

Now that we have laid the basic groundwork for an
analytical model of man, we are able to begin our
analysis of will power. Let us first concern ourselves
with the question of where will comes from. To begin
with, we all know that each of the previously analyzed
aspects of our being appears to exert some will force
during each day of our lives. When our bodies are
hungry, tired, or yearning for sex, there is a real force
being exerted. A force which attempts to compel us
toward satisfying these needs. For even if we do not
wish to eat at just that moment, the body generally
pesters us until we finally give in. Thus, we say "the
body has a will of its own." Depending upon which
will power is greater—the one consciously guided by
inner reason, or the one automatically generated by the
body's animal drives—determines what action actually
takes place.

But our emotions also seem to display "a will of
their own." Most of us have, at times, found ourselves
shrouded by emotions of fear or jealousy which we
intellectually recognized as foolish and even detrimental
to our well-being. Yet it is very difficult, without
much training, to exert enough consciously controlled
will power to expel these negative emotional vibrations.
So, again, we see a battle between will power generated
by a lower aspect of our being and the will which we
intentionally apply at any given moment.

Furthermore, the same analysis holds for our

thoughts. Most of us exercise virtually no control over our thought patterns. In fact, most people think it inconceivable that we all could develop the will power necessary to have *complete control* over what thoughts pass before our consciousness every single moment of every day. The main problem, here, is that we have become so identified with our thoughts—especially the EGO thought patterns of "I and mine"—that we never step back to realize that there is an aspect of "You" totally distinct from these thoughts which potentially has full control over them. Most of us, however, have had times when the "whining" inside became so foolish and absurd that we internally stepped back and said, "Be still!"

Thus, by means of these few examples we are able to see that all aspects of our lower self (body, emotions, and thoughts) display varying degrees of will power. It is by this means that they command our attention and demand that certain actions take place. But we also see that "You," the aspect distinct from body, emotions, and thoughts, can exert will power in an attempt to rise above these lower-self-dictated conditions. Which of these aspects has the greater will power determines every feature of our behavior. So we can see that when we learn to exercise our conscious will more fully, we actually become "advanced beings." We are finally able to rise above the animal drives which govern the behavior of all lower animals, as well as control emotions and thoughts, in order to come into tune with our Higher Aspect.

Interestingly enough, as we gradually put forth the necessary effort to increase the power of our conscious will, we discover that the will force of our lower aspects simultaneously decreases. For example, if we have a desire which continually bothers us, we find that the more we strengthen our conscious will by rising above it, the less often this desire is able to command our attention. Indeed, we find that there is actually a trade-off between the amount of will flowing to these different aspects at any given moment. The reason for this observed trade-off characteristic of the will force is that *in the purest sense all will power finds its origin in the same reservoir.* As we proceed with the analysis we shall come to see that this reservoir of will coincides with Higher Self (consciousness). *That is, will power is an intrinsic quality of consciousness, and, thus, wherever consciousness is located, so also do we find the will force.*

To see how this works, let us say the body has a minor injury and is exerting its own will power to complain about the discomforts. We all know that if we can manage to withdraw our attention from the body, we will no longer be conscious of the pain. If we dwell upon body consciousness, however, the complaints become greater and greater. In the former case, we have withdrawn the will force from the body by using it at higher levels. In the latter case, when we were concentrating upon the body, we increased the body's command over will power by focusing our consciousness there. This same analysis holds true at the emotional and mental levels. *To whatever degree we hold our consciousness on any given aspect of our being, this determines the degree of will force which is made available to that aspect.*

What we must realize now is that we have spent so much time fully identifying with body, emotions, and thoughts that a habit-formed flow of consciousness, and, thus, will power, goes to these aspects at all times. In other words, there are two distinct states of the will force within each man: habit-formed will and consciously-directed will. The difference being that habit-formed will is directed subconsciously and consciously-directed will is directed consciously. But it must be emphasized that it is really the same, one will force being distributed at these different levels.

Following directly from this we should be able to see all of the inner conflict which takes place each day as one of habit-formed will versus consciously-directed will. It thus becomes apparent that this inner conflict represents an amazing waste of power. Both sides of the battle, lower self and Higher Self, are receiving all of their strength from the same reservoir. In order to get an idea of the size of this reservoir, think for a moment how strong the body's will can be. Then add to this the even more stubborn force exerted by our emotions, and further, the forces displayed by EGO and SUPEREGO thought patterns. Finally, we note that in times of conflict, when all of these lower self aspects are acting up simultaneously, there is still that tremendous degree of will which "You" have exerted from time to time to overcome these inner traumas. Add together all of these forces, rather than having them oppose one another, and imagine how much will power potentially is available to us. With that force harnessed, a man can accomplish anything which he sets his mind to, and can do so in a state of absolute peace. All that is required is to reclaim will in the name of Higher Self, and then to carry out each and every action on the basis of reason-guided will, rather than habit-formed will.

It should be noted that this harnessed will force is one of the greatest powers in Creation. Just by looking at our own personal experiences we are able to see that will has the power to direct activity at the physical, emotional, and mental levels. For example, since each bodily movement represents the expenditure of either conscious or subconscious will, this means that will actually has the power to move atoms. Furthermore, we all carry out the process of thinking—the creating and holding of specific thought-forms—by means of this same will force.

But it is not just aspects of our own being which can be influenced by our will. For example, the practice of hypnosis represents one man's will power dominating that of another's. In this condition the hypnotist's will not only can control the movement of the other man's body, but also can dictate his thoughts and emotions. And hypnosis is not the only example of this phenomenon. We have numerous cases throughout history of men who have had the ability to cause strictly physical objects to move merely by applying sufficient will power.* If we could harness our wills there would be no limit to the feats which could be performed. Thus, it is written, in the literal sense: "If ye have faith, and doubt not ... ye shall say unto this mountain, Be thou removed, and be thou cast into the sea, it shall be done." [Matthew 21:21]

How to Develop Will

The development of will power is a gradual, natural process. The important point to be remembered is that *will is developed by exercising it.* Each and every time we take advantage of that split second between stimulus and response, we are laying the pattern for successive applications of will to come more easily. Soon we get into the good habit of never acting without first tuning in to the rational guidance from within. And practices which quiet the mind, such as daily meditation, make it so that instead of a split second lull between stimulus and habit-formed response, we have a much longer period. We eventually get to the point where we are always acting from this "Conscious Center"—while observing external conditions, while taking the time to apply our reason, as well as while actually responding to the situation itself. Once we reach this state we finally become "conscious beings." No longer are we merely automatons whose every physical, emotional, and mental activity is run by habit.

*Modern scientific research studies this under the label of "psychokinesis."

It should be emphasized that this state can be reached only by building our will force on a day-to-day basis. "Spiritual aids" such as hypnosis and drugs *cannot* permanently raise us to a higher center of consciousness. It is true that sometimes they can jolt us into a higher center on a temporary basis, but the moment external conditions get heavy, we fall right back down. This is because we did not build our growth upon a solid foundation. Once the will force is developed, however, it is then available under all conditions throughout life.

Thus, the development of a strong, reason-guided will is an essential requisite for permanently attaining higher states of consciousness. We should never let a moment of our lives pass where we are not in complete awareness of, and have potential control over, all of the lower aspects of our being. It is quite similar to training a horse—if the rider's will is not stronger than the horse's, no training can take place. The truth is, however, that most of our "lower self" horses are completely out of control. We must gently and gradually—while maintaining full patience, love, and respect for their basic nature—break our lower selves of their habit-formed will and train them to respond fully to our higher, consciously-directed will. Only in this way can we attain the permanent sense of peace and freedom which we are inwardly seeking.

The Relation Between Man's Will and God's Will

Having developed a workable model of the will force, we now are able to turn our attention to a question lacking formal analysis for far too long—"What exactly is the relation between 'man's will' and 'God's will'?" To begin with we note that almost all religious teachings, as well as our own intuitive perceptions, tell us that man has "free will." That is, man is a "free moral agent" who has full control over all actions which he carries out. In the same religious doctrines, however, we are also taught that at the source of Creation is an omnipresent, omniscient, omnipotent Intelligence which is generally called "God." In a previous work we have shown that this Intelligence necessarily displays the qualities of both consciousness and energy, and, as such, can be referred to as "Conscious Energy." If all of Creation is made manifest by means of this Supreme Consciousness ordering the underlying Energy Field, then this means God's will is responsible for the movement and non-movement of every atom in Creation. In fact, God's omnipresence stems from the fact that He *is* the electrons, neutrons, and protons which make up the atom itself. He *is* the underlying homogeneous Energy Field which physicists are rapidly coming to realize is behind all aspects of Creation.

How, then, can man have "free will?" If this omni-present, omniscient, omnipotent force is at every moment creating, preserving, and destroying different aspects of His Creation, how can anything exist which is divorced from His will? One can readily see that if for one second this Conscious Energy removed its will power from maintaining any aspect of Creation, that aspect would cease to exist. The atoms would fly apart, lacking the directed energy which holds them together. Nothing can take place but by His will, and, thus, anything which is separated from His will would cease to exist. So it appears the more we say about this underlying Intelligent Force, the more we realize that the concept of man's "free will" is totally illogical in a Universe held together from moment to moment by God's omnipotent will. How, then, do we reconcile this apparent conflict?

Employing the model of the will force constructed earlier, we recall that we identified the source of man's will power as Higher Self (consciousness). We further showed that since will power is the force which directs the flow of consciousness, whenever our awareness falls upon body, emotions, or thoughts a proportionate amount of the will force becomes focused there. For this reason, if we wish more fully to understand the source of man's will power, we must first carefully study the source of his consciousness—for these two aspects flow together.

The source of man's consciousness has been examined in our previous work, *The Search for TRUTH*. We shall, therefore, not enter into a formal proof at this time. Let it suffice to say that the Higher Self (soul) aspect of our being *is* Pure Conscious Energy.

Furthermore, we know that behind every aspect of Creation lies this same omnipresent, omniscient, omnipotent field of Conscious Energy. Combining these statements about man and God, we finally are able to see the true meaning of the Biblical passage, "Man is created in the image of God." God is *Pure Universal Consciousness, and the individual consciousness of any one soul is only a focal point of this Universal Spirit.* Figure 3 (next page) should help us to see this more clearly.

In this figure we have three men depicted such that the area crossed by the dotted lines represents their lower selves—body, emotions, and mind. At this level the men are separate entities, each one fully centered in an "I—you" frame of reference. Moving back to the three vertices, the "points" represent their souls, that is, the consciousness which becomes aware of all activity at the physical, emotional, and mental levels. In fact, the soul is often referred to as the "Eternal Witness." This is because the "point" never actually goes out into the area of dotted lines, it merely observes all activity occurring within that area. But so much time is spent watching this outer area—and generally no time just "being the center"—that this Pure Consciousness has become hypnotized into thinking, "I am my body, I am my emotions, I am my thoughts."

As high as this soul level is, however, it should be noted that even here the three men are still distinct. Each man has a unique center (focal point) from which his consciousness watches the lower aspects of Creation.

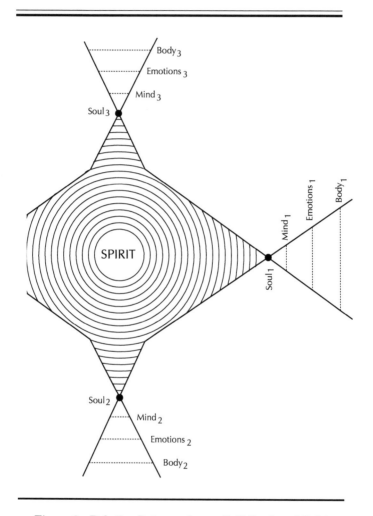

Figure 3—Relation Between Lower Self, Soul, and Spirit

But what is this soul made of and where did it come from? These questions can be answered by taking another step back in Figure 3 in order to see that the same Universal Consciousness (i.e., Spirit) is behind all men's individualized consciousnesses. *Each man's soul is merely a specific focal point of the omnipresent Spirit.*

Thus, there are three distinct states of consciousness—lower self, soul, and Spirit. And the truth of the above analysis need not be limited to the strength of this, or any other, intellectual argument. Any man who exerts the necessary effort to rise above his lower self can experience these Higher Aspects for himself. After all, they form the very essence of our Inner Being.

Now that we have taken the time to examine the origin of man's consciousness and to reveal the exact relation between lower self, soul, and Spirit, we can return to questioning the relation between God's will and man's "free will." In the analysis just completed we saw that Higher Self (man's consciousness), which was earlier described as the source of man's will power, has as its source the Universal Consciousness itself. Since will power is an intrinsic quality of consciousness, it follows that the true origin of the will force must also be found in this Universal Spirit. In other words, as God's Infinite Consciousness shines forth into many "soul rays" of individualized consciousnesses, we also get a focusing of the Universal Will into man's will. Then, by virtue of identification with lower self, consciousness and will are brought down to the mental, emotional, and physical levels. So we now are formally able to see that there is but one will behind all of Creation. *What we call man's will is really God's will which has become concentrated into an individual focal point for each separate soul.*

In order to see exactly how this works, and how we can so strongly feel that we are exercising "free will," let us draw an analogy from the dream state. To begin with, we know that our dreams are constructed purely of "mind stuff," and that the vast majority of them are a manifestation of our own subconscious mind. Each and every object present in our dreams is constructed of the same substance—our own consciousness. It is easily seen that nothing can exist in a dream, nor any action take place, but that it is initiated from this subconscious center. Furthermore, when the subconscious expresses its latent desires through our dreams, it does so by exercising subconscious will. This will power is the motivating force behind the creation, preservation, and destruction of all aspects of our dreams.

Thus, to our own dream world we are "God"—i.e., our consciousness and will are the sole power behind the entire dream creation. Yet it is also true that the various "dreamed-persons" who interact in the dream do so as though they had "free will." Is it not true that when you are interacting *in* your dream, you feel pretty much the same way as when you are interacting in the waking world? You are faced with external problems, and even have all the internal conflicts which characterize waking life. If in your dream you find yourself in a situation which requires an important choice to be made, you generally sit down, weigh the pros and cons, and finally come to a decision. Beyond any doubt you feel as though you have "free will" in all your activities while interacting in the dream state.

But this time we can plainly see the error in this apparent freedom. As discussed above, every object, feeling, thought, and action which takes place in your dream is the direct result of "you-the-dreamer" expressing yourself at the subconscious level. It is *your* will, at this higher level, which creates every situation in the dream world, *not* the will of the dreamed-persons themselves. There is only one consciousness and one will force in the entire system. It is *your* consciousness and *your* will which has formed itself into the varied aspects of the dream world.

This analogy is well worth considerable contemplation. The relation between the "dreamed-persons" and "you-the-dreamer" is exactly the relation that exists between you and God. For example, from the perspective of your dream world you are omnipresent. It is your consciousness which composes the most basic unit of the entire dream structure. Returning to the waking world, this is analogous to how God's Conscious Energy composes the omnipresent substance behind every atom in Creation. Furthermore, in relation to your dream world you are also omniscient and omnipotent. As discussed above, nothing can take place in your dreams except that you subconsciously will it. At this level you are totally aware of, and have absolute control over, all activity within the dream sequence. *It is your unified field of consciousness and will power which is behind all of the seemingly individualized consciousnesses of the various dreamed-persons.* This is exactly the relation that exists between God and His Creation.

Coming into Tune with Universal Will

So we see that our concept of "free will" is really the result of the illusionary state which our minds are in. It is only because our self-concept (EGO) separates us from the Universal Consciousness that we are able to separate our will from the Universal Will. But how are we to employ this knowledge in our everyday lives? Should we just sit back and rationalize away our activities by attributing them to the Higher Will? What we shall see is that this line of reasoning is actually a hindrance rather than an aid to our spiritual growth.

While we are living in the illusion of separateness, we must work from where we are in order to attain Higher Realization. Because of identification with body, emotions, and mind we have automatically surrendered some of our will force to these lower aspects. If one day we suddenly intellectually come to realize the illusionary nature of our "free will," and decide to "surrender to the flow of life," we are apt to find ourselves flowing with lower self rather than Higher Self. The habit-formed patterns set due to ego-consciousness are right now in the driver's seat. If we attempt to surrender our conscious will, these patterns will be free to carry out their habit-formed actions.

Before any true blending of our individualized will with the Universal Will can occur, we must first reclaim our will force in the name of Higher Self. Then, once lower self is trained and we have reasonable control over body, emotions, and mind, surrender of our will to the Universal Will becomes the quickest path to Universal Consciousness. Once our ego-desires are worn away, then, and only then, can we be sure that the directions in which life is leading us are patterned directly by the Higher Guidance. Otherwise we are apt to be projecting subconscious ego-desires which will have the effect of patterning our lives from this lower level.

Thus, for the most part, the Path is a gradual one. As we step-by-step free our will force from lower self's control, we continuously increase our attunement with the Universal Will. As we come into tune with the Infinite Will, by providing a clear channel through which It can express itself, we begin to experience directly our balance with all of Nature. In every situation we get an inner intuitive signal of what to do and what to say, which always yields optimal long-run results. The more we seriously wish to live for the Infinite, instead of for the finite, the more we come to know the Universal Will. But the first step is to learn to exercise our individual will ceaselessly and fearlessly, based upon conscious reasoning. Only in this way does our will become our own. We must build our will into a dynamic force which is capable of carrying out the Universal Will under all circumstances. This is done by ceaselessly affirming, no matter what obstacles confront us, *"I can, and I will!"* Then comes the total surrender of this dynamic will to the Infinite Intelligence who alone knows how best to use it. The state must be reached where one can say in all sincerity, as did the Master, "Not my will, but Thy will be done."

THE
LAW
OF
LOVE

The Law of Love

*Love has to spring spontaneously from within and is in no way
amenable to any form of inner or outer force. Love and
coersion can never go together. But though love cannot be
forced on anyone, it can be awakened in him through love itself.
Love is essentially self-communicative—those who do not have it
catch it from those who have it. True love is unconquorable and
irresistable, and it goes on gathering power and spreading itself
until eventually it transforms everyone whom it touches.*

—Meher Baba

The Nature of the Love Force

One of the cornerstones of Eastern philosophy is the
seven *chakras*. These seven vital centers, located in the
astral body of man, have for thousands of years
played a major role in mystical literature. For this
reason it is not surprising that the *chakras* provide the
perfect foundation upon which to build our model of
the love force. In order to carry out this study,
however, we must first become familiar with the
locations and basic functions of these *chakras*.

Figure 4 presents a simple chart listing the Western
and Eastern names of the *chakras* and their positions
corresponding to the human body. Figure 5 shows the
chakra system diagrammatically. It should be emphasized
that since these psychic centers do not actually exist on

English Name	Sanskrit Name	Situation
Root or Basic Chakra	Mūlādhāra	At the base of the spine
Spleen or Splenic Chakra	•	Over the spleen
Navel or Umbilical Chakra	Manipūra	At the Navel, over the solar plexus
Heart or Cardiac Chakra	Anāhata	Over the heart
Throat or Laryngeal Chakra	Vishuddha	At the front of the throat
Brow or Frontal Chakra	Ājnā	In the space between the eyebrows
Crown or Coronal Chakra	Sahasrāra	On top of the head

Source: C. W. Leadbeater, *The Chakras*, Wheaton, Ill.:
Theosophical Publishing House, 1972, p. 7.

Figure 4—Location of the *Chakras*

the physical plane, the locations given here are only the
physical counterpart of the astral *chakras*. It should
also be made clear that whenever using the term
"astral," we are referring to that rate of energy vibration at which "emotions" exist. That is, the actual
feelings of fear, hate, friendship and desire do not exist
on the physical plane, for emotions themselves are not
composed of atoms. The term generally used to denote

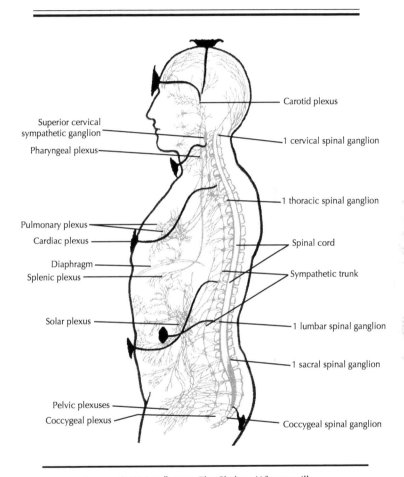

Source: C. W. Leadbeater, *The Chakras*, Wheaton, Ill.:
Theosophical Publishing House, 1972, p. 40.

Figure 5—The *Chakras* and the Nervous System

the plane on which these subtler aspects do exist is the "astral plane."

So we already have a basis for understanding the first important function of the *chakras*. The fact that they exist on the astral plane, which is the emotional rate of vibration, indicates that they must be intricately tied in with the operation of our emotions. We are taught by those with sufficiently well developed astral senses (i.e., those with a high degree of extrasensory perception) that the seven *chakras* are, in fact, the centers through which we receive our emotions. Each specific emotion is made manifest by a unique vibration rate at the astral level, and it is via these *chakras* that "we," the conscious receiver, become aware of these emotional vibrations. But this role of emotional sensory mechanism is only one of the functions of the psychic centers.

The other main function of the *chakras* is that of storehouse and relay station for the energy (*prana*) which flows throughout our physical, emotional, and mental aspects. In an earlier work* we discussed at length the means by which man receives the energy expended during each day's physical, emotional, and mental activities. We concluded that besides the physical energy sources of food, air, and sunlight, man also has the ability to tap energy directly from the Infinite Source. Yogic science tells us it is in chan-

*Michael A. Singer, *The Search for TRUTH*, Alachua, Fla.: Shanti Publications, 1974, pp. 85-88.

neling this higher flow of energy that the *chakras* play a vital role.

Yoga teaches that the *prana* (life-force) enters the system through the *medulla oblongata*, located at the back of the neck where the spine meets the brain.* This medullary center is actually the polar opposite of the brow *chakra* (Spiritual Eye), and, thus, forms one end of the force field which is the sixth *chakra*.

After entering in through the medulla, the energy habitually flows down the spine and is stored in the root *chakra*. When this stored force, which yogis call "*kundalini*," attempts to climb back up the spine to be expended, generally it is unable to do so because of blockages which exist in the *chakras*. These blockages of the higher psychic centers are the direct result of the low rate of emotional vibrations which man entertains. That is, since these seven psychic centers play the dual role of (1) sensing our emotional vibrations and (2) relaying the energy flow, it follows that the level of our emotions will affect the level of the energy flow, and vice versa. It is upon this revealed interdependence of emotions and energy flow that we shall construct our Law of Love.

The first step in our analysis is to realize that when the energy flow is centered mainly in the first *chakra*, at the base of the spine, our level of consciousness is determined by the properties of this center. Examining these properties, we find that the desires associated

*See: Paramahansa Yogananda, *Autobiography of a Yogi*, Los Angeles: Self-Realization Fellowship, 1972, p. 422fn.

with the root *chakra* are the most basic of all human drives—the animal instincts. Preoccupation with food, clothing, and shelter, at the absolute minimum level necessary for the sustenance of life, paints the picture of a man who is living totally for "self." All emotional and mental energies are focused at this lower level, creating a blockage of the higher motives which all men are capable of displaying. Once the emergency of sustaining the body's well-being is passed, however, the man has time to look outside of "self" and aim his motivating, desire-directed energies at a more social level. This expansion of consciousness is equivalent to the clearing of *chakra* number one, and at least some energy then is permitted to climb into the second *chakra*.

This second center, however, is just one small step removed from the first. It too is concerned primarily with animal drives. This time they are our animal drives which require interaction to be fulfilled—such as the basic sex drive and the resultant desire for a family unit. It is well known that preoccupation with sexual desires can limit a man's scope of consciousness and forbid him from experiencing the more evolved levels of human interaction. One whose mind is always thinking of sex comes to relate to all women as sex objects, and all men as competitors. Wherever this person goes, and whomever he meets, his relations are automatically held to a lower level. This is all due to this one desire which colors and distorts conscious perceptions. Most men, however, have managed to rise above the dictates of the sex force, and, in doing so, have cleared the channels to the third *chakra*.

The level of consciousness associated with the third psychic center is concerned with a much broader scope of human interaction. The desires manifest in this center are generally beyond those directly related to our animal aspect. Perhaps the best term to describe the third *chakra* is "ego-consciousness." In this state man is motivated by his higher desires of group accept-ance, superiority, achievement, and so on. All we need do is look into our daily actions to get a good idea of what characterizes the third *chakra*. For it is from this center of consciousness that we are generally operating.

With this *chakra* being so familiar to all of us, let us take a moment to see what specific emotional vibra-tions are blocking the energy flow at this level. Here, we have all of the emotions of pride, jealousy, hate, insecurity, guilt, possessiveness, self-consciousness, and the like. The common feature being that all these emotional vibrations are concerned mainly with our-selves and the current state of our interactions with the outside world. The fact that all these emotions do reflect back on ourselves is why they have the effect of limiting our scope of consciousness. As in the case of the second *chakra*, we again have the situation where most of the man's physical, emotional, and mental activities are circling around one group of interests—in this case, ego-desires. Undoubtedly, this set of desires is less limiting than a comparative preoccupation with the sexual desire. But, nonetheless, these ego-desires do hold our scope of consciousness to a specific field of activity. In general, we can say that the trademark of the third *chakra* is "self." All physical, emotional, and mental activity is motivated by the drive to satisfy our own ego-desires.

In drastic contrast to this state is the level of consciousness which unfolds once the energy flow reaches the heart *chakra*. As one might imagine, this fourth center is associated with the motivating force which men call "love." Thus, we already have uncovered a basic truth of the love force: *True love, being made manifest in the fourth center of conscious-ness, can only exist once the limiting pull of EGO is transcended.* That is to say, love is *not* the emotional state of: "I love her because she's pretty and it will reflect well on me. I love him because he can provide for me a secure family life. I love her because she stimulates me intellectually." Nor even, "I love him because we have lived together for so long that I would be helpless without him." These are all ego-centered desires, and, as such, do not reflect the pure love force. In fact, many relationships which we term "love" are really motivated by the third *chakra*. They are so self-oriented that the energy flow is totally unable to become manifest in the higher centers.

From time to time, however, we have all experi-enced at least a partial opening of the heart center. There are those times when we first meet a loved one and get totally swept off our feet. We actually feel a "melting of the heart," as if warm sensations were flowing in this area. And, in fact, this is exactly what is happening. For all of the characteristics of this love state are caused directly by energy flowing through the fourth *chakra*. When an event occurs in our lives which is sufficiently strong to remove our consciousness from self-oriented desires, energy is free to spurt upward into the higher centers. *It is this awakening of the heart* chakra, *along with all of the ensuing physical, emotional, and mental effects, which is being referred to when using the word "love."*

Qualities of the Love Force

Love is *self-sufficient.* Having seen the true nature of love, and having examined the metaphysics behind its existence, we now are able to study some important qualities of this force. To begin with, we should note that *love is a totally internal force which in no way is dependent upon any specific outside events for its existence.* For example, due to the relation of aural vibrations, two individuals may find themselves suddenly "melting in love" while in each other's company. Although this experience is quite overwhelming, one must be careful not to confuse the stimulus of the love reaction with the reaction itself. The girl whom we "fall in love with" only plays the part of having sufficiently strong vibrations that our minds be taken off our self-centered thoughts and emotions and aimed toward her. This expansion of consciousness beyond the confines of "self" allows the energy to climb to a higher center, and love is felt. Thus, love is a force which always exists within us, and, as such, in no way is dependent upon any particular person or experience for its existence.

Perhaps the easiest way to see this is to think of our general state of mind when we have just "fallen in love." During these blissful periods we are so thoroughly engrossed in love that it seems we are in love with every person we meet. In this state it is difficult to say just whom we are in love with, for we actually can come to feel just as strong stimulations of the love force for many other people as we did for the person who initially opened the fourth *chakra*. Further, while that *chakra* is open we can also feel the same love vibration for all of Nature. If we see a flock of birds fly by—again we feel pulsations of the "divine nectar" flowing through us. This can even happen with roadside flowers, or even a rock. Once that *chakra* is cleared, and we are "in love" (as being "in water"), then we are *in it*, regardless of what happens in the outside world. But most of us still have the tendency of associating this feeling with the person who initially turned us on to this state of love consciousness.

Be this as it may, there is one experience which beyond any doubt shows the autonomous nature of the love force. Many who practice meditation have had the experience of sitting alone in a candlelit room, thinking of nothing but the technique of meditation, when all of a sudden sensations beyond imagination begin to fill their being. The heart melts ... characteristic tingling sensations shoot throughout the body ... tears begin to flow ... and an indescribably blissful experience is generated.

The explanation for this inner experience can be found with the ancient yogic seers of India. Its occurrence is just one of the many steps along the Path to Universal Consciousness. For what we shall see is that yoga is the science of *how* to systematically clear the *chakras* in order that we be able to raise the energy up the spine at will. In other words, the opening of the fourth *chakra* can be brought about directly by scientifically clearing the lower centers. Once this is accomplished the sensations which follow are the same as those characteristic of "falling in love." This time, however, we have the perplexing problem of deciding just *who* it is we are in love with! For this time we have tuned in to the love force without the need of any external catalyst.

The true beauty of this experience is that the more often we open the heart *chakra*, and keep the lower *chakras* free from emotional debris, the more often we are able to "live in love" during the course of our everyday lives; until finally we reach the point of feeling love for everyone. In this state the slightest kind word, friendly gesture, or beauty of Nature opens the *chakras* and melts us again and again in love. This is pure love. It is in no way attached to, or dependent upon, any specific outside events. As such, our love for those around us is not contingent upon our own desires or expectations concerning their behavior. We are just "in love," fully immersed in the fourth *chakra*. This quality of love's independence from worldly events inspired the poet Gibran to write, "Love is sufficient unto love."*

Love is Unconditional. A second important quality of the love force is that pure love is unconditional. If our feelings toward another person in any way are dependent upon certain behavior on their part, then this is ego-love. It is a love based upon expectations, and expectations are generated by our own concept of what would be most pleasing to us. Thus, it is an "I love you for what you can do for me," and not a pure "I love you." It should be obvious at this point that a relationship based upon expectational love cannot generate the levels of soul gratification that can be attained in a pure love relationship. If we are always judging another's behavior, based upon our own concept of desired behavior, there is a total blockage of the third *chakra*. Both individuals are afraid to be themselves fully, and each one is putting on the mask which they think the other person wants to see. The vast majority of the time not only does this expectational role-playing limit the growth of a true relationship, but our concept of what would be most pleasing to the other person is generally wrong anyway.

In drastic contrast to this expectational love, truly

*Kahlil Gibran, *The Prophet*, New York: Alfred A. Knopf, 1973, p. 13.

unconditional love is when someone loves "You," the aspect deep inside trying her best to play a role or wear a mask. The "You" who wants to please, and wants to be loved—not the personality which "You" hide behind. To most of us the very notion of letting down the mask and standing naked before the world is most frightening and beyond consideration. We fear being taken advantage of or hurt through rejection. For if one's personality is rejected, he can always alter the mask in order to find acceptance. But if "You" reveal yourself as you really are—what then? No place to hide.

Despite all of these inner fears of removing the mask, it should be clear that when someone loves your personality and merely accepts you for the roles you are playing—it is not the real "You" who are receiving the benefit of this acceptance. There is always the fear of failure and the tensions created due to not being yourself fully at all times. Nevertheless, as hard as it may seem for some to believe, there does exist a love in which one can love "You" directly. That is, one can love "You" regardless of how you look, what you say, or what you do. When a person loves "You," they understand the meaninglessness of how you externally express yourself. It becomes a standing game between you to watch your lower selves "do their thing," while a part of you remains detached, winking at one another in the midst of the worldly melodrama. This is true acceptance. With it comes the absolute sense of freedom in knowing that the relationship is an eternal one.

There is nothing that can come between you, because you know each other as you really are.

So, here we have unconditional love. Absolutely no anxiety or insecurity is possible at this level. You have stood naked before one another, stripped of all masks, and have seen the enormous similarity between your True Selves. Only in this way can you learn to "love your neighbor as you love yourself"—accepting every aspect of his behavior. For you now understand the causes of that behavior and have learned to look beyond the "act" in order to focus upon the "actor." Unfortunately, few ever know this level of love. A love where one does not *have to* give of his body, nor be careful to sound intelligent in conversations. *In unconditional love, you are just loved because you are "You."*

Love is Non-Possessive. Following directly from this, another important requisite of the love force is that *true love is non-possessive.* Love need not be attached to any single person or place, and, in truth, any attempts to "hold" love will result in its dissipation. It is our own ego-insecurities which feel, "I'm loved today, but what about tomorrow? What should I do to ensure my security in the relationship?" This type of thought blocks the heart *chakra* and holds the entire relationship to a lower self level.

In contrast, if one is not attached to any external objects for his love, he can freely give and receive love without feeling the need to possess another person. In these situations there is room for true growth in the relationship. If both individuals are whole, content in their own inner peace and love, they can have a truly high relationship sharing these internal feelings. But if a person is lacking these inner qualities, he tries to find a substitute for them in his external environment. In this situation he is "in need" and is capable only of extracting from the other person that which he feels will satisfy his needs. In no way is he capable of truly giving, only taking.

So it becomes evident that the surest way to improve our relations with other people is to first improve our relations with our self. The security which is sought by trying to possess another person generally leads to its own failure. In trying to hold on too tight, we create a cage for the other person and will always lose them—if not physically, then at the higher levels where it really matters. The space must be of a fair size for two souls to grow together in love. For no matter how close we become, no two souls walk the same Path. The aspect of love comes from *sharing* each other's Path, not by trying to force each other to walk the same Path.

Love is Beyond the Body. One should never think that love can be saved for that "special person." Love is a flow, and if you stop that flow awaiting an expectation of tomorrow, you are like a dried-up riverbed which is incapable of properly channeling the love force. But if you give your love to all, under all circumstances, you come to know love and become one with love. When you meet that "special person" with whom you wish to share your life, you then are able to give freely of the river of love which has come to flow continually through you.

But one must be careful not to confuse love with sexual desires. In the purest sense love has nothing to do with bodies, either separately or together. Love is way beyond the physical, although it is capable of being expressed through the world of atoms. What often happens is that the sensations of energy flowing through the fourth *chakra* become so overwhelming we can hardly contain them. So we seek to express this energy on the physical plane by channeling it through our bodies. This is perhaps the purest motive for sex, and the combined love of the two people actually can build the energy force and reach new heights through this mutual expression. If we are to be honest with ourselves, however, we know that most sex is not this pure. As with all other activities motivated by the third *chakra*, sex carried out to gain acceptance, relief from boredom, or to generate a feeling of security tends to block the channels needed for the full manifestation of the love force. Yet, we are so used to trying to express our inner feelings through the body that love without sex seems almost unnatural.

Nevertheless, we need only touch for a moment the point of unconditional love for all of humanity to realize there must be another way to express ourselves. We obviously cannot engage in sex with everyone.

What happens is that slowly but surely we begin to mature in love. We find that by allowing the love force to quietly remain within us, it begins to blossom. The love energy which is not expended in a physical expression forms the seeds from which grows deeper and deeper realizations of true love. This love force then begins to express itself in every word, action, and thought throughout our lives. Unable specifically to aim its expression at one individual's body, this love force rapidly grows until it seeks to find expression in any way possible. Once this state is reached, every task begins to yield the same blissful waves of love that previously required bodily contact.

So, time and again we see that love is an inner force which is not to be erroneously tied to any one individual. On the contrary, if the love is truly pure, it will automatically share itself unconditionally and non-possessively with all individuals.

Love and Marriage

Having come to understand the source and meaning of true love, we naturally are faced with the question of the relation between love and marriage. We have seen that, in the ultimate, a man who has progressed well along the Path of Life will attain the state where he sees all as equal, and, thus, loves all equally. But does this mean that the institution of marriage should fall by the wayside? To the contrary. Under these conditions marriage finally can come to provide the stable, positive environment which is so needed for individual and societal growth.

Sharing our Path with a loved one, and finding the expression for our love in the form of children, is one of the greatest gifts that life has to offer. To be totally pure, however, the relationship must be based solely upon the sharing of the love force which already flows within each partner. If the marriage represents a means of financial and social security, or the fulfillment of the ego-desire to play the role of "having a husband and children," then the marital environment is not optimal for soul growth. Under these conditions there are preconceived notions of what is expected of the relationship, and these notions put boundaries around the free expression of the love force. We must be willing to accept whatever direction the relationship takes, and this requires absolute security in ourselves. Only if we are whole and content with ourselves can we feel comfortable in allowing the relationship to follow its natural course. Though this state may not exist at the moment, it must be striven for and clearly seen as the goal of each individual. The idea that marriage means dependence, possessiveness, financial security, and so on must be put aside if the true heights of the relationship are to be explored. In essence, the key word for a Higher Self marriage is "sharing," nothing more. And we can only share what we already have. We cannot expect the relationship miraculously to create the inner peace and contentment which we have failed to establish within ourselves.

Most importantly, we should constantly keep in mind what love really is. For some of us may find ourselves in a marriage where love once seemed to exist, but now it is gone. Generally, both individuals are certain that it is changes in the other person that caused the love to die out. But let us take the time to analyze what really has occurred in these cases. In the early stages of our relationship with a loved one, we have the situation where our vibrations are so new and positive to one another that we knock each other completely out of our everyday egocentricity. That is, while in each other's presence we completely forget our everyday problems and focus on higher thoughts. This has the effect of clearing the *chakras*, and we find ourselves "in love." So now, feeling that this is the person obviously meant for us, we spend more and more time with them, and perhaps even get married.

Over time, a very interesting phenomenon occurs. We spend so much time sharing our lives that the other person, in essence, becomes our everyday life. They are the ones with whom we share our sexual life, we share our financial ups and downs with them, they are the major part of our social life, and they even partake in our hours of leisure. So it naturally happens that their vibration tends to become more "everydayish," and, thus, loses its power to sweep us out of our daily emotional melodrama.

Once this happens, we have slipped into a third *chakra* relationship and the initial feelings of overpowering love become less and less frequent. Then,

suddenly, one day we find ourselves meeting a new
acquaintance—a secretary, golf pro, friend's cousin—
and we unexpectedly begin melting in the vibration of
love. We become confused, feeling we have lost our
love for our husband, and since all we ever wanted to
do was to remain "in love," we begin to spend time
with the other person.

It should be noted that this entire problem was
allowed to become manifest solely due to our misunder-
standing of the love force. It is most natural that a
new external vibration should pull us out of our everyday emotional pattern, and, thus, allow the energy flow
to enter the fourth *chakra*. It is nothing to be ashamed
of, nor is it in any way being unfaithful to our spouse.
Love is to be shared with all. If we bother to expend
the necessary self-effort to keep our *chakras* open, we
will be able to feel this blissful sensation every moment
of our lives. The problems come about only due to our
erroneous notions of having to "own" the person who
originally stimulated the energy flow, as well as to our
habit-formed desires to express our love physically. If
we would just accept love for a new acquaintance for
what it is—a tuning in to the love force within us—then
perhaps we could go home and share this newly
stimulated love with our own marriage partner.

Thus, we see that we cannot blame our spouse for
the dwindling of the love feeling within us. It is not
part of the marriage vows that one promises to keep
the other person's fourth *chakra* open. Each person
must do the necessary inner work to keep their own

love force flowing. To allow ourselves to be totally dependent upon external vibrations in order to transcend our egocentricity tends to lead to either a dying off of the love force or a very unstable marriage due to sporadic relations with "new acquaintances." All this can be avoided, however, and the full manifestation of the love force continually experienced, by vowing to ourselves to work daily on clearing our own emotional and mental waste matter. This is accomplished through regular periods of meditation, accompanied by any other scientific methods of self-improvement.

It cannot be stressed enough—love dwells within us. We must go directly inside to find a permanent, ever-expanding place "in love." It is not fair to hold another person responsible for our love force. What will happen is, as our vibrations begin to get accustomed to one another's, there will come the need for more and more external excitement—anything new, anything to take our minds off of the everyday vibration. It drives so many marriages under, and what is worse, it takes the individuals with it. So we should all be able to see by now that it is the timeless wisdom of sages and seers which offers the only really meaningful "marriage counseling:" *Love, peace, contentment, security—they are all inner forces, so seek them within.*

The Love for God

A state does exist, however, when marriage is unnecessary. When one comes to see the love force for what it really is, he loses the need to focus the sharing of it on any one individual. To the man who has trained his mind to see things as they *really* are—a manifestation of the one Energy Source behind Creation—all things become one. Whatever he sees is in terms of atoms being held together by energy bonds, and all movement of these atoms being directly generated by the Energy Force itself. If he finds his love force stimulated by a beauty of Nature, he sees through the illusionary veil of Creation and focuses his love on that Conscious Energy which at every moment is creating, preserving, and destroying all the different aspects of Creation. If his eyes should happen to fall upon a stunningly beautiful woman, his mind again focuses on the miraculous Energy Force which is arranging mere electrons, protons, and neutrons so they are manifest in such an exquisite form. There is no longer a need for sex or any other physical expression of the love force. This man dwells in a state of divine rapture every moment of his life. There are no sensations which can enter in through the five physical senses which in any way can measure up to the Bliss which saturates the entire being of one who lives with open *chakras.*

The very act of training the mind to "see Creation with seeing eyes" has the effect of permanently extricating ourselves from the entire worldly melo-drama. Once we see that all things are really manifes-tations of the one, omnipresent, omniscient Force Field, how, then, can we entertain the notions of good and evil, beautiful and ugly, wanted and unwanted?

Since all is one, we learn to accept it all. And, more importantly, we learn to love it all. We begin to love God, the Intelligent Force holding it all together.

This love for God cannot be "learned" in Sunday School, nor can it be instilled based solely upon the fear of Scriptural Writings. Love for the Infinite comes about naturally as one begins to focus their daily awareness on the scientifically supported realities of the Universe, rather than on the illusions of the senses. Thinking in terms of the infinitesimal place which we hold in the Universal Structure has the effect of rapidly humbling EGO. How can pride, fear, or jealousy exist in a mind which continuously dwells in the thought of the Infinite? In this mental environment EGO begins to fall away, and with this comes the clearing of the *chakra* system. The individual naturally associates the flow of the love force with that which stimulated it—in this case, "the Infinite." And the more we think along these lines, the more we permanently live "in love."

So we see that the love for God is the only really pure love. It has the qualities of (1) always being manifest, due to the omnipresent nature of the Infinite Intelligence, (2) being totally unconditional, since She is the one who is behind both good and evil, and (3) being free from the restricting feeling of possessiveness, since She is equally manifest in all aspects of Creation. Let there be no doubt that the man who has put out the necessary effort to see beyond the illusion of Creation rests in an eternal blanket of love and peace, unassailable by any force on Earth.

The Higher Chakras

Thus far, we have painted the picture of a very high state attainable by all men. In contrast to our everyday lives, however, this state of permanently dwelling in the fourth *chakra* appears to be almost a fairytale. But the most amazing feature of this state is that it represents only the fourth *chakra*. This means that there are three more centers which are associated with even higher states of consciousness.

Beginning our brief exploration of the higher three centers, we note that the stimulation of the fifth *chakra* (the throat *chakra*) represents the full evolvement of man's mental aspect. Just as energy focusing in the fourth center (the heart center) represents the highest emotional vibrations—unconditional love—so energy focusing in the fifth center represents the highest mental state—wisdom. But wisdom should not be confused with knowledge. A knowledgeable man can know all about the relations of cause and effect which yield our laws of physics, chemistry, biology, and psychology. But the man of wisdom sees *beyond* the forces of cause and effect, always focusing upon the Energy Source from which it all flows. By the sheer development of his mental capacity he is able to transcend the trickery of the physical senses and relate directly to the one Reality. *Thus, we see that in the fifth center of consciousness our mental capacity is expanded to the point where we are able to understand the true nature of Creation, and live that Truth every moment of our lives.*

In turn, this state of wisdom provides the necessary environment for clearing the blockages to the sixth *chakra.* A man who continually uses his advanced mental powers to discern the underlying Energy everywhere, at all times, soon comes to identify himself more and more with this Energy. It is a quality of the mind that whatever it spends its time focusing upon becomes its object of identification. When our minds are fixed in the state of body consciousness, we live under the delusion, "I am my body." But when this same mind comes to focus continually upon the omnipresent Energy, it begins to intuitively feel, "I am Energy." Once this identification is complete, the soul then is freed of all attachment to body, emotions, and mind. For, in truth, the soul *is* Conscious Energy—an individual portion of the Universal Conscious Energy.* So when the mind becomes freed from its lower self identification, it takes on the quality of a flawless mirror, able to reflect perfectly the true nature of the soul. It is this stilling of the mind which actually permits the energy to flow into the sixth *chakra. Thus, the sixth* chakra *is associated with soul consciousness, and in this state the soul is able to perceive itself directly as pure Conscious Energy.*

To make this even clearer, let us recall that earlier we stated that man's energy flow enters his system through the medullary center and then flows down the spine. We have thus far in this analysis shown the

*See Figure 3, p. 54.

states of consciousness experienced as this energy begins to work its way back up the spine and focuses in the five different spinal *chakras.* In contrast to this, the state of consciousness associated with the sixth center is that of the energy *before* it ever passes down the spine.

Keeping this in mind, recall that the sixth *chakra* has two poles—the medullary center in the back of the neck and the brow center (Spiritual Eye) between the two eyebrows. When the Conscious Energy entering in through the medullary center is brought forward to the Spiritual Eye, rather than allowing it to pass down the spine to the lower *chakras,* a beautiful Light begins to shine in this forehead area.* As we spend more and more time meditating on this Light, we intuitively come to realize, "I am this Light." In very truth, this is the "Light of the soul," for the soul is Light (i.e., energy). So with the sixth *chakra* open we are able to perceive directly our own true nature—we are the Light which has "taken on the flesh." What is more, we are able to see now that the exact method by which we "take on the flesh" is by Conscious Energy passing down the spine and identifying with the lower centers therein.

Finally, in the same way that the sixth *chakra* represents the direct intuitive perception of soul consciousness, so the seventh *chakra* represents the state of Universal Consciousness. Having come to transcend

---

*"And they shall see his face; and his name *shall be* in their foreheads. And there shall be no night there; and they need no candle, neither light of the sun; for the Lord God giveth them light: . . ." [Revelation 22:4-5]

all illusionary identification with body, emotions, and mind, the soul spends more and more time focusing upon itself. It must be emphasized that this is not an intellectual state, but a direct realization of the Higher Truth. Once fully identified with the Inner Light, the further realization is reached that, "This Light Energy which I AM is the same Light Energy which is behind all souls and behind every atom in Creation." This final, complete identification with the one Absolute Source is the state of Universal Consciousness. This state is associated with "the thousand petaled Lotus" at the top of the head (the seventh *chakra*), and represents the goal of the entire process of evolution.

Love—The Highest Path

The subject of the evolutionary advancement of consciousness is beyond the scope of the current text. In our study of the *chakra* system, however, we have uncovered a rough guideline of what is required of man to fulfill his part in this consciousness expansion. It should be clear by now that whether we are aware of it or not, we are all gradually advancing in this direction. The operation of the Law of Karma, as explained in our first essay, has the overall effect of presenting us with the lessons needed to rise above our lower selves and progress toward Enlightenment. In essence, the equilibrium force of the system as a whole is gradually guiding the evolutionary movement on an ever advancing Path to expanded consciousness.

Plants and lower animals have no choice but to allow Cause and Effect (i.e., interaction with their environment) to bring about the changes necessary for advancement to take place. Once we reach the human kingdom, however, things are quite different. Man is endowed both with reason and a sufficiently well developed will force so that he is able to use the Law of Karma consciously to accelerate his evolution. For example, an animal may be overcome suddenly by the urge to kill solely for the passion of killing. If the circumstances provide a suitable victim, the act will be carried out and corresponding *sanskaras** created. When the same urge strikes a human, however, there is that split second available for the application of reason-guided will. He is provided with the choice of giving in to his animal passions, or applying sufficient will power to rise above them.

Thus, by always acting upon principles representing higher motives of behavior, man consciously can avoid the creation of "bad *sanskaras.*" As was stressed in our essay on will, this means that proper use of the will force can be a major aid in our soul's evolution. The man who consciously exercises reason-guided will can work off existing karma more rapidly, while at the same time avoiding the accumulation of negatively binding *sanskaras*.

However, this constant struggle to overcome lower self by the proper application of the will force is *not*

---

*For a definition of the term *sanskara*, see p. 20.

the Ultimate Path to Enlightenment. It is true that man's consciously-directed will is potentially strong enough to win the battle against lower self's habit-formed will, but *forcing* the mind to obey its master is quite a difficult task. What is more, this attempt to force the mind can, in and of itself, create a great deal of tension and uneasiness. In contrast to this "battle method," based upon the Law of Will, we turn now to the "devotional method," based upon the Law of Love.

Once we have applied sufficient will force to step back and view lower self as distinct from ourselves, we then have the foundation upon which the love method can be developed. Note that in this case we need not have full control over lower self, just the realization that we do not wish to devote our lives to his endless desires. Thus, we are left facing the question of the basic reason for living each and every day of our lives.

Understanding that there is but one Intelligent Force behind all that we see, this question of life's meaning becomes almost rhetorical. The rational move becomes to devote our lives to God. We renounce our "little self" (EGO) in order to surrender to the overall purpose of Creation. Over time, this love and devotion for the Infinite has the effect of focusing our whole being into a state of one-pointedness. Just as when we fall in love with a friend, we have no problem thinking about them day and night, so when we fall in love with God, we find our thoughts continually levitating toward Him. This clearing of EGO's mental and emotional debris affects the opening of the fourth *chakra* and the blissful sensations become so great that all thought ceases. But this time thought has been transcended, not due to the application of tremendous will power, but due to the level of ecstasy being reached.

Thus, we can totally overcome lower self without the need of constantly battling with him. All that is needed is to develop true love and devotion for our Ultimate Goal, and then the love force will automatically draw us to our Destination. Just as the will force can supercede the slow, mechanical operations of karma, love can pass beyond the will force. *Once devotion* (Bhakti) *is developed, the aspirant then can surrender himself fully to the Infinite and be assured he will be evolving on the most rapid Path to Enlightenment.*

*   *   *   *   *

Karma, Will, and Love—three Universal Laws governing the process of evolution. Three stepping-stones aiding the soul on its Path to the Infinite.

Peace Be With You

Suggested Readings

Arnold, Sir Edwin, translator. *Bhagavad-Gita (The Song Celestial)*. Wheaton, Ill.: The Theosophical Publishing House, 1970.

Barnett, Lincoln. *The Universe and Dr. Einstein*. New York: Bantam Books (Science and Mathematics edition), 1957.

Bucke, Richard Maurice. *Cosmic Consciousness*. New York: E. P. Dutton and Company, Inc., 1969.

Einstein, Albert. *Ideas and Opinions*. New York: Crown Publishers, Inc., 1954.

Gibran, Kahlil. *The Prophet*. New York: Alfred A. Knoph, 1973.

Isherwood, Christopher. *Ramakrishna and His Disciples*. London: Methuen and Co. Ltd. (distributed by Vedanta Press), 1965.

Leadbeater, C. W. *Man Visible and Invisible*. Wheaton, Ill.: The Theosophical Publishing House, 1971.

Meher Baba. *Discourses*. San Francisco: Sufism Reoriented Inc., 1971.

Meher Baba. *God Speaks*. New York: Dodd, Mead and Company, 1973.

Meher Baba. *Meher Baba on Love*. Meher Baba Center, Poona, India: Meher Era Publications, 1972.

Ram Dass. *Be Here Now*. San Cristobal, New Mexico: Lama Foundation, 1971.

Ram Dass. *The Only Dance There Is*. New York: Anchor Press, 1974.

Singer, Michael A. *The Search for TRUTH*. Alachua, Fla.: Shanti Publications, 1974.

Swami Muktananda Paramahansa. *Chitshakti Vilas (The Play of Consciousness)*. Ganeshpuri, India: Shree Gurudev Ashram, 1972.

Swami Sri Yukteswar. *The Holy Science*. Los Angeles: Self-Realization Fellowship, 1972.

Yogananda, Paramahansa. *Autobiography of a Yogi*. Los Angeles: Self-Realization Fellowship, 1972.

Yogananda, Paramahansa. *The Law of Success*. Los Angeles: Self-Realization Fellowship, 1970.

Michael Singer is founder and director of Temple of the Universe in Alachua, Florida, a spiritual center which is centered around the teachings.

By the Same Author

The Search for
TRUTH

Michael A. Singer

This book is for those who, like the astronauts, cannot look at this view of our planet without asking, "WHY?" The search conducted within these pages is a logical journey into the fields of biology, psychology, physics, parapsychology, yogic science, and Eastern and Western religious philosophies. Are they merely viewing different aspects of the same Truth?

"Prior to reading this work I had absolutely no idea of what the 'New Spiritual Movement' was all about, nor what it meant to 'alter one's state of consciousness.' This logically based, scientifically supported analysis finally makes it possible for the Western intellectual to view the contribution of the East from his own rational-minded perspective. What is more, many of the truths presented in this work are so deep that they quickly find their way into everyday life and can never again be ignored. I recommend *The Search for TRUTH* to all truth seekers—young and old."

—*Irving J. Goffman Ph.D; former chairman, Department of Economics*
University of Florida; Gainesville, Florida
Deputy Assistant Secretary, HEW under President Ford

"I have been in the psychic field for over 40 years now, and have given and received innumerable lectures and have read a multitude of books. So often in my work the situation has arisen as to what to recommend to the interested intellectual who simply 'doesn't believe.' *The Search for TRUTH* provides that long sought bridge between the 'scientist' and the 'spiritualist.' It is truly a masterpiece."

—*Reverend Eloise Page, Psychic Counselor*
President of the Spiritual Camp
Cassadega, Florida

The Search for TRUTH by Michael A. Singer
Shanti Publications, Inc., 5200 NW 43rd Street, Suite 102-384
Gainesville, FL 32606